EXULTATIONS

EXULTATIONS

OF

EZRA POUND

LONDOŃ

ELKIN MATHEWS, VIGO STREET

M CM IX

HASKELL HOUSE PUBLISHERS Ltd.

Publishers of Scarce Scholarly Books

NEW YORK. N. Y. 10012

1973

HASKELL HOUSE PUBLISHERS Ltd.
Publishers of Scarce Scholarly Books
280 LAFAYETTE STREET
NEW YORK. N. Y. 10012

Library of Congress Cataloging in Publication Data

Pound, Ezra Loomis, 1885–
    Exultations of Ezra Pound.

    Poems.
    I.   Title.
PS3531.082E9   1973   811'.5'2   72-10016
ISBN 0-8383-1683-2

TO

CARLOS TRACY CHESTER

" amicitiae longaevitate "

I HAVE to thank the Editors of the *English Review* and the *Evening Standard* and *St. James's Gazette* for permission to include in this volume certain poems which originally appeared in those papers.

CONTENTS

EXULTATIONS

Guido invites you thus [1]

" LAPPO I leave behind and Dante too,
    Lo, I would sail the seas with thee alone!
Talk me no love talk, no bought-cheap fiddl'ry,
Mine is the ship and thine the merchandise,
All the blind earth knows not th' emprise
Whereto thou calledst and whereto I call.

Lo, I have seen thee bound about with dreams,
Lo, I have known thy heart and its desire;
Life, all of it, my sea, and all men's streams
Are fused in it as flames of an altar fire!

Lo, thou hast voyaged not! The ship is mine."

[1] The reference is to Dante's sonnet " Guido vorrei . . . "

Night Litany

O DIEU, purifiez nos cœurs!
       purifiez nos cœurs!

Yea the lines hast thou laid unto me
       in pleasant places,
And the beauty of this thy Venice
       hast thou shown unto me
Until is its loveliness become unto me
       a thing of tears.

O God, what great kindness
       have we done in times past
       and forgotten it,
That thou givest this wonder unto us,
       O God of waters?

O God of the night
       What great sorrow
Cometh unto us,
       That thou thus repayest us
Before the time of its coming?

O God of silence,
       Purifiez nos cœurs,
       Purifiez nos cœurs,
For we have seen
The glory of the shadow of the
    likeness of thine handmaid,

Yea, the glory of the shadow
    of thy Beauty hath walked

Upon the shadow of the waters
    In this thy Venice.
                And before the holiness
Of the shadow of thy handmaid
    Have I hidden mine eyes,
                O God of waters.

O God of silence,
                Purifiez nos cœurs,
                Purifiez nos cœurs,
O God of waters,
                make clean our hearts within us
And our lips to show forth thy praise,
                For I have seen the
Shadow of this thy Venice
Floating upon the waters,
                And thy stars
Have seen this thing out of their far courses
Have they seen this thing,
                O God of waters,
Even as are thy stars
Silent unto us in their far-coursing,
Even so is mine heart
    become silent within me.

                Purifiez nos cœurs
O God of the silence,
                Purifiez nos cœurs
O God of waters.

11

Sandalphon

The angel of prayer according to the Talmud stands unmoved
among the angels of wind and fire, who die as their one song is
finished, also as he gathers the prayers they turn to flowers in his
hands.

A ND these about me die,
    Because the pain of the infinite singing
Slayeth them.
Ye that have sung of the pain of the earth-horde's
        age-long crusading,
Ye know somewhat the strain,
    the sad-sweet wonder-pain of such singing.
And therefore ye know after what fashion
This singing hath power destroying.

Yea, these about me, bearing such song in homage
Unto the Mover of Circles,
Die for the might of their praising,
And the autumn of their marcescent wings
Maketh ever new loam for my forest;
And these grey ash trees hold within them
All the secrets of whatso things
They dreamed before their praises,
And in this grove my flowers,
Fruit of prayerful powers,
Have first their thought of life
                And then their being.

Ye marvel that I die not! *forsitan*!
Thinking me kin with such as may not weep,
Thinking me part of them that die for praising
—yea, tho' it be praising,
past the power of man's mortality to
dream or name its phases,
—yea, tho' it chant and paean
past the might of earth-dwelt
soul to think on,
—yea, tho' it be praising
as these the winged ones die of.

Ye think me one insensate
                else die I also
Sith these about me die,
And if I, watching
Ever the multiplex jewel, of beryl and jasper
                        and sapphire
Make of these prayers of earth ever new flowers;
Marvel and wonder!
Marvel and wonder even as I,
Giving to prayer new language
And causing the works to speak
Of the earth-horde's age-lasting longing,
Even as I marvel and wonder, and know not,
Yet keep my watch in the ash wood.

Sestina: Altaforte

LOQUITUR: *En* Bertrans de Born.
   Dante Alighieri put this man in hell for that he was a stirrer-
   up of strife.
   Eccovi!
   Judge ye!
   Have I dug him up again?
The scene is at his castle, Altaforte. "Papiols" is his jongleur.
The Leopard," the *device* of Richard (Cœur de Lion).

I

DAMN it all! all this our South stinks peace.
   You whoreson dog, Papiols, come! Let's to
      music!
I have no life save when the swords clash.
But ah! when I see the standards gold, vair, purple,
      opposing
And the broad fields beneath them turn crimson,
Then howl I my heart nigh mad with rejoicing.

II

In hot summer have I great rejoicing
When the tempests kill the earth's foul peace,
And the light'nings from black heav'n flash crimson,
And the fierce thunders roar me their music
And the winds shriek through the clouds mad, opposing,
And through all the riven skies God's swords clash.

III

Hell grant soon we hear again the swords clash!
And the shrill neighs of destriers in battle rejoicing,
Spiked breast to spiked breast opposing!

14

Better one hour's stour than a year's peace
With fat boards, bawds, wine and frail music!
Bah! there's no wine like the blood's crimson!

IV

And I love to see the sun rise blood-crimson.
And I watch his spears through the dark clash
And it fills all my heart with rejoicing
And pries wide my mouth with fast music
When I see him so scorn and defy peace,
His lone might 'gainst all darkness opposing.

V

The man who fears war and squats opposing
My words for stour, hath no blood of crimson
But is fit only to rot in womanish peace
Far from where worth's won and the swords clash
For the death of such sluts I go rejoicing;
Yea, I fill all the air with my music.

VI

Papiols, Papiols, to the music!
There's no sound like to swords swords opposing,
No cry like the battle's rejoicing
When our elbows and swords drip the crimson
And our charges 'gainst "The Leopard's" rush clash.
May God damn for ever all who cry "Peace!"

VII

And let the music of the swords make them crimson!
Hell grant soon we hear again the swords clash!
Hell blot black for alway the thought "Peace"!

Piere Vidal Old

It is of Piere Vidal, the fool par excellence of all Provence, of
whom the tale tells how he ran mad, as a wolf, because of his love
for Loba of Penautier, and how men hunted him with dogs through
the mountains of Cabaret and brought him for dead to the dwelling
of this Loba (she-wolf) of Penautier, and how she and her Lord
had him healed and made welcome, and he stayed some time at
that court. He speaks:

WHEN I but think upon the great dead days
    And turn my mind upon that splendid madness,
Lo! I do curse my strength
And blame the sun his gladness;
For that the one is dead
And the red sun mocks my sadness.

Behold me, Vidal, that was fool of fools!
Swift as the king wolf was I and as strong
When tall stags fled me through the alder brakes,
And every jongleur knew me in his song,
And the hounds fled and the deer fled
And none fled over long.

Even the grey pack knew me and knew fear.
God! how the swiftest hind's blood spurted hot
Over the sharpened teeth and purpling lips!
Hot was that hind's blood yet it scorched me not
As did first scorn, then lips of the Penautier!
Aye ye are fools, if ye think time can blot

From Piere Vidal's remembrance that blue night.
God! but the purple of the sky was deep!
Clear, deep, translucent, so the stars me seemed
Set deep in crystal; and because my sleep
—Rare visitor—came not,—the Saints I guerdon
For that restlessness—Piere set to keep

One more fool's vigil with the hollyhocks.
Swift came the Loba, as a branch that's caught,
Torn, green and silent in the swollen Rhone,
Green was her mantle, close, and wrought
Of some thin silk stuff that's scarce stuff at all,
But like a mist wherethrough her white form fought,

And conquered! Ah God! conquered!
Silent my mate came as the night was still.
Speech? Words? Faugh! Who talks of words and
      love?!
Hot is such love and silent,
Silent as fate is, and as strong until
It faints in taking and in giving all.

Stark, keen, triumphant, till it plays at death.
God! she was white then, splendid as some tomb
High wrought of marble, and the panting breath
Ceased utterly. Well, then I waited, drew,
Half-sheathed, then naked from its saffron sheath
Drew full this dagger that doth tremble here.

Just then she woke and mocked the less keen blade.
Ah God, the Loba! and my only mate!
Was there such flesh made ever and unmade!

God curse the years that turn such women grey!
Behold here Vidal, that was hunted, flayed,
Shamed and yet bowed not and that won at last.

And yet I curse the sun for his red gladness,
I that have known strath, garth, brake, dale,
And every run-way of the wood through that great
        madness,
Behold me shrivelled as an old oak's trunk
And made men's mock'ry in my rotten sadness!

No man hath heard the glory of my days:
No man hath dared and won his dare as I:
One night, one body and one welding flame!
What do ye own, ye niggards! that can buy
Such glory of the earth? Or who will win
Such battle-guerdon with his "prowesse high"?

O Age gone lax! O stunted followers,
That mask at passions and desire desires,
Behold me shrivelled, and your mock of mocks;
And yet I mock you by the mighty fires
That burnt me to this ash.

   .   .   .   .   .   .

Ah! Cabaret! Ah Cabaret, thy hills again!
   .   .   .   .   .

Take your hands off me! . . .   [*Sniffing the air.*
                    Ha! this scent is hot!

Ballad of the Goodly Fere[1]

Simon Zelotes speaketh it somewhile after the Crucifixion.

HA' we lost the goodliest fere o' all
    For the priests and the gallows tree?
Aye lover he was of brawny men,
O' ships and the open sea.

When they came wi' a host to take Our Man
His smile was good to see,
"First let these go!" quo' our Goodly Fere,
"Or I'll see ye damned," says he.

Aye he sent us out through the crossed high spears
And the scorn of his laugh rang free,
"Why took ye not me when I walked about
Alone in the town?" says he.

Oh we drank his "Hale" in the good red wine
When we last made company,
No capon priest was the Goodly Fere
But a man o' men was he.

I ha' seen him drive a hundred men
Wi' a bundle o' cords swung free,
That they took the high and holy house
For their pawn and treasury.

           1 Fere = Mate, Companion.

They'll no' get him a' in a book I think
Though they write it cunningly;
No mouse of the scrolls was the Goodly Fere
But aye loved the open sea.

If they think they ha' snared our Goodly Fere
They are fools to the last degree.
"I'll go to the feast," quo' our Goodly Fere,
"Though I go to the gallows tree."

"Ye ha' seen me heal the lame and blind,
And wake the dead," says he,
"Ye shall see one thing to master all:
'Tis how a brave man dies on the tree."

A son of God was the Goodly Fere
That bade us his brothers be.
I ha' seen him cow a thousand men.
I have seen him upon the tree.

He cried no cry when they drave the nails
And the blood gushed hot and free,
The hounds of the crimson sky gave tongue
But never a cry cried he.

I ha' seen him cow a thousand men
On the hills o' Galilee,
They whined as he walked out calm between,
Wi' his eyes like the grey o' the sea.

20

Like the sea that brooks no voyaging
With the winds unleashed and free,
Like the sea that he cowed at Genseret
Wi' twey words 'spoke' suddently.

A master of men was the Goodly Fere,
A mate of the wind and sea,
If they think they ha' slain our Goodly Fere
They are fools eternally.

I ha' seen him eat o' the honey-comb
Sin' they nailed him to the tree.

** *The Publisher desires to state that the "Ballad of the Goodly Fere"—by the wish of the Author—is reproduced exactly as it appeared in the "English Review."*

Hymn III

From the Latin of Marc Antony Flaminius, sixteenth century.

A S a fragile and lovely flower unfolds its gleaming
    foliage on the breast of the fostering earth, if
    the dew and the rain draw it forth;
So doth my tender mind flourish, if it be fed with the
    sweet dew of the fostering spirit,
Lacking this, it beginneth straightway to languish,
    even as a floweret born upon dry earth, if the
    dew and the rain tend it not.

Sestina for Ysolt

THERE comes upon me will to speak in praise
Of things most fragile in their loveliness;
Because the sky hath wept all this long day
And wrapped men's hearts within its cloak of grey-
ness,
Because they look not down I sing the stars,
Because 'tis still mid-March I praise May's flowers.

Also I praise long hands that lie as flowers
Which though they labour not are worthy praise,
And praise deep eyes like pools wherein the stars
Gleam out reflected in their loveliness,
For whoso look on such there is no greyness
May hang about his heart on any day.

The other things that I would praise to-day?
Besides white hands and all the fragile flowers,
And by their praise dispel the evening's greyness?
I praise dim hair that worthiest is of praise
And dream upon its unbound loveliness,
And how therethrough mine eyes have seen the stars.

Yea, through that cloud mine eyes have seen the stars
That drift out slowly when night steals the day,
Through such a cloud meseems their loveliness

23

Surpasses that of all the other flowers.
For that one night I give all nights my praise
And love therefrom the twilight's coming greyness.

There is a stillness in this twilight greyness
Although the rain hath veiled the flow'ry stars,
They seem to listen as I weave this praise
Of what I have not seen all this grey day,
And they will tell my praise unto the flowers
When May shall bid them in in loveliness.

O ye I love, who hold this loveliness
Near to your hearts, may never any greyness
Enshroud your hearts when ye would gather flowers,
Or bind your eyes when ye would see the stars;
But alway do I give ye flowers by day,
And when day's plucked I give ye stars for praise.

But most, thou Flower, whose eyes are like the stars,
With whom my dreams bide all the live-long day,
Within thy hands would I rest all my praise.

Portrait

From "La Mère Inconnue."

NOW would I weave her portrait out of all dim
      splendour.
Of Provence and far halls of memory,
Lo, there come echoes, faint diversity
Of blended bells at even's end, or
As the distant seas should send her
The tribute of their trembling, ceaselessly
Resonant. Out of all dreams that be,
Say, shall I bid the deepest dreams attend her?

Nay! For I have seen the purplest shadows stand
Alway with reverent chere that looked on her,
Silence himself is grown her worshipper
And ever doth attend her in that land
Wherein she reigneth, wherefore let there stir
Naught but the softest voices, praising her.

"Fair Helena" by Rackham

" What I love best in all the world?"

WHEN the purple twilight is unbound,
    To watch her slow, tall grace
                and its wistful loveliness,
And to know her face
                is in the shadow there,
Just by two stars beneath that cloud—
The soft, dim cloud of her hair,
And to think my voice
                can reach to her
As but the rumour of some tree-bound stream,
Heard just beyond the forest's edge,
Until she all forgets I am,
And knows of me
Naught but my dream's felicity.

Laudantes Decem Pulchritudinis
Johannae Templi

I

WHEN your beauty is grown old in all men's
        songs,
And my poor words are lost amid that throng,
Then you will know the truth of my poor words,
And mayhap dreaming of the wistful throng
That hopeless sigh your praises in their songs,
You will think kindly then of these mad words.

II

I am torn, torn with thy beauty,
O Rose of the sharpest thorn!
O Rose of the crimson beauty,
Why hast thou awakened the sleeper?
Why hast thou awakened the heart within me,
O Rose of the crimson thorn?

III

The unappeasable loveliness
        is calling to me out of the wind,
And because your name
        is written upon the ivory doors,
The wave in my heart is as a green wave, unconfined,
Tossing the white foam toward you;

And the lotus that pours
Her fragrance into the purple cup,
Is more to be gained with the foam
Than are you with these words of mine.

IV

He speaks to the moonlight concerning the Beloved.

Pale hair that the moon has shaken
Down over the dark breast of the sea,
O magic her beauty has shaken
About the heart of me;
Out of you have I woven a dream
That shall walk in the lonely vale
Betwixt the high hill and the low hill,
Until the pale stream
Of the souls of men quench and grow still.

V

Voices speaking to the sun.

Red leaf that art blown upward and out and over
The green sheaf of the world,
And through the dim forest and under
The shadowed arches and the aisles,
We, who are older than thou art,
Met and remembered when his eyes beheld her
In the garden of the peach-trees,
In the day of the blossoming.

VI

I stood on the hill of Yrma
    when the winds were a-hurrying,

With the grasses a-bending
    I followed them,
Through the brown grasses of Ahva
    unto the green of Asedon.
I have rested with the voices
    in the gardens of Ahthor,
I have lain beneath the peach-trees
    in the hour of the purple:

Because I had awaited in
    the garden of the peach-trees,
Because I had feared not
    in the forest of my mind,
Mine eyes beheld the vision of the blossom
There in the peach-gardens past Asedon.

O winds of Yrma, let her again come unto me,
Whose hair ye held unbound in the gardens of Ahthor!

<h2 style="text-align:center">VII</h2>

Because of the beautiful white shoulders and the
    rounded breasts
I can in no wise forget my beloved of the peach-trees,
And the little winds that speak when the dawn is
    unfurled
And the rose-colour in the grey oak-leaf's fold

When it first comes, and the glamour that rests
On the little streams in the evening; all of these

Call me to her, and all the loveliness in the world`
Binds me to my beloved with strong chains of gold.

VIII

If the rose-petals which have fallen upon my eyes
And if the perfect faces which I see at times
When my eyes are closed—
Faces fragile, pale, yet flushed a little, like petals of
    roses:
If these things have confused my memories of her
So that I could not draw her face
Even if I had skill and the colours,
Yet because her face is so like these things
They but draw me nearer unto her in my thought
And thoughts of her come upon my mind gently,
As dew upon the petals of roses.

IX

He speaks to the rain.

O pearls that hang on your little silver chains,
The innumerable voices that are whispering
Among you as you are drawn aside by the wind,
Have brought to my mind the soft and eager speech
Of one who hath great loveliness,

Which is subtle as the beauty of the rains
That hang low in the moonshine and bring
The May softly among us, and unbind
The streams and the crimson and white flowers and
    reach
Deep down into the secret places.

X

The glamour of the soul hath come upon me,
And as the twilight comes upon the roses,
Walking silently among them,
So have the thoughts of my heart
Gone out slowly in the twilight
Toward my beloved,
Toward the crimson rose, the fairest.

Aux Belles de Londres

I AM aweary with the utter and beautiful weariness
And with the ultimate wisdom and with things
    terrene,
I am aweary with your smiles and your laughter,
And the sun and the winds again
Reclaim their booty and the heart o' me.

Francesca

YOU came in out of the night
    And there were flowers in your hands,
Now you will come out of a confusion of people,
Out of a turmoil of speech about you.

I who have seen you amid the primal things
Was angry when they spoke your name
In ordinary places.
I would that the cool waves might flow over my
      mind,
And that the world should dry as a dead leaf,
Or as a dandelion seed-pod and be swept away,
So that I might find you again,
Alone.

Greek Epigram

DAY and night are never weary,
  Nor yet is God of creating
For day and night their torch-bearers
The aube and the crepuscule.

So, when I weary of praising the dawn and the sun-
      set,
Let me be no more counted among the immortals;
But number me amid the wearying ones,
Let me be a man as the herd,
And as the slave that is given in barter.

Christophori Columbi Tumulus

From the Latin of Hipolytus Capilupus, Early Cent. XVI.

GENOAN, glory of Italy, Columbus thou sure
    light,
Alas the urn takes even thee so soon out-blown.
Its little space

Doth hold thee, whom Oceanus had not the might
Within his folds to hold, altho' his broad embrace
Doth hold all lands.

Bark-borne beyond his bound'ries unto Hind thou wast
Where scarce Fame's volant self the way had cast.

Plotinus

A S one that would draw through the node of things,
   Back sweeping to the vortex of the cone,
 Cloistered about with memories, alone
In chaos, while the waiting silence sings:

Obliviate of cycles' wanderings
   I was an atom on creation's throne
   And knew all nothing my unconquered own.
God! Should I be the hand upon the strings?!

But I was lonely as a lonely child.
I cried amid the void and heard no cry,
And then for utter loneliness, made I
New thoughts as crescent images of *me*.
And with them was my essence reconciled
While fear went forth from mine eternity.

On His Own Face in a Glass

O STRANGE face there in the glass!
    O ribald company, O saintly host,
O sorrow-swept my fool,
What answer? O ye myriad
That strive and play and pass,
Jest, challenge, counterlie?
I? I? I?
            And ye?

Histrion

NO man hath dared to write this thing as yet,
  And yet I know, how that the souls of all men
    great
At times pass through us,
And we are melted into them, and are not
Save reflexions of their souls.
Thus am I Dante for a space and am
One François Villon, ballad-lord and thief
Or am such holy ones I may not write,
Lest blasphemy be writ against my name;
This for an instant and the flame is gone.

'Tis as in midmost us there glows a sphere
Translucent, molten gold, that is the "I"
And into this some form projects itself:
Christus, or John, or eke the Florentine;
And as the clear space is not if a form's
Imposed thereon,
So cease we from all being for the time,
And these, the Masters of the Soul, live on.

The Eyes

REST Master, for we be a-weary, weary
    And would feel the fingers of the wind
Upon these lids that lie over us
Sodden and lead-heavy.

  Rest brother, for lo! the dawn is without!
The yellow flame paleth
And the wax runs low.

Free us, for without be goodly colours,
Green of the wood-moss and flower colours,
And coolness beneath the trees.

  Free us, for we perish
In this ever-flowing monotony
Of ugly print marks, black
Upon white parchment.

  Free us, for there is one
Whose smile more availeth
Than all the age-old knowledge of thy books:
And we would look thereon.

Defiance

YE blood-red spears-men of the dawn's array
   That drive my dusk-clad knights of dream away,
Hold! For I will not yield.

My moated soul shall dream in your despite
A refuge for the vanquished hosts of night
That *can* not yield.

Song

LOVE thou thy dream
All base love scorning,
Love thou the wind
And here take warning
That dreams alone can truly be,
For 'tis in dream I come to thee.

Nel Biancheggiar

BLUE-GREY, and white, and white-of-rose,
  The flowers of the West's fore-dawn unclose.
I feel the dusky softness whirr
Of colour, as upon a dulcimer
" Her " dreaming fingers lay between the tunes,
As when the living music swoons
But dies not quite, because for love of us
—knowing our state
How that 'tis troublous—
It wills not die to leave us desolate.

Nils Lykke

BEAUTIFUL, infinite memories
    That are a-plucking at my heart,
Why will you be ever calling and a-calling,
And a-murmuring in the dark there?
And a-reaching out your long hands
Between me and my beloved?

And why will you be ever a-casting
The black shadow of your beauty
On the white face of my beloved
And a-glinting in the pools of her eyes?

A Song of the Virgin Mother

In the play " Los Pastores de Belen."

From the Spanish of Lope de Vega.

A S ye go through these palm-trees
O holy angels;
Sith sleepeth my child here
Still ye the branches.

O Bethlehem palm-trees
That move to the anger
Of winds in their fury,
Tempestuous voices,
Make ye no clamour,
Run ye less swiftly,
Sith sleepeth the child here
Still ye your branches.

He the divine child
Is here a-wearied
Of weeping the earth-pain,
Here for his rest would he
Cease from his mourning,
Only a little while,
Sith sleepeth this child here
Stay ye the branches.

Cold be the fierce winds,
Treacherous round him.
Ye see that I have not
Wherewith to guard him,
O angels, divine ones
That pass us a-flying,
Sith sleepeth my child here
Stay ye the branches.

Planh for the Young English King

That is, Prince Henry Plantagenet, elder brother to Richard " Cœur de Lion."

From the Provençal of Bertrans de Born "Si tuit li dol eíh plor elh marrimen."

IF all the grief and woe and bitterness,
  All dolour, ill and every evil chance
That ever came upon this grieving world
Were set together they would seem but light
Against the death of the young English King.
Worth lieth riven and Youth dolorous,
The world o'ershadowed, soiled and overcast,
Void of all joy and full of ire and sadness.

Grieving and sad and full of bitterness
Are left in teen the liegemen courteous,
The joglars supple and the troubadours.
O'er much hath ta'en Sir Death that deadly warrior
In taking from them the young English King,
Who made the freest hand seem covetous.
'Las! Never was nor will be in this world
The balance for this loss in ire and sadness!

O skilful Death and full of bitterness,
Well mayst thou boast that thou the best chevalier
That any folk e'er had, hast from us taken;
Sith nothing is that unto worth pertaineth
But had its life in the young English King,
And better were it, should God grant his pleasure
That he should live than many a living dastard
That doth but wound the good with ire and sadness.

From this faint world, how full of bitterness
Love takes his way and holds his joy deceitful,
Sith no thing is but turneth unto anguish
And each to-day 'vails less than yestere'en,
Let each man visage this young English King
That was most valiant mid all worthiest men!
Gone is his body fine and amorous,
Whence have we grief, discord and deepest sadness.

Him, whom it pleased for our great bitterness
To come to earth to draw us from misventure,
Who drank of death for our salvacioun,
Him do we pray as to a Lord most righteous
And humble eke, that the young English King
He please to pardon, as true pardon is,
And bid go in with honouréd companions
There where there is no grief, nor shall be sadness.

Alba Innominata

From the Provençal.

IN a garden where the whitethorn spreads her
    leaves
My lady hath her love lain close beside her,
Till the warder cries the dawn—Ah dawn that
    grieves!
Ah God! Ah God! That dawn should come so soon!

"Please God that night, dear night should never
    cease,
Nor that my love should parted be from me,
Nor watch cry 'Dawn'—Ah dawn that slayeth peace!
Ah God! Ah God! That dawn should come so soon!

"Fair friend and sweet, thy lips! Our lips again!
Lo, in the meadow there the birds give song!
Ours be the love and Jealousy's the pain!
Ah God! Ah God! That dawn should come so soon!

"Sweet friend and fair take we our joy again
Down in the garden, where the birds are loud,
Till the warder's reed astrain
Cry God! Ah God! That dawn should come so soon!

48

" Of that sweet wind that comes from Far-Away
Have I drunk deep of my Belovéd's breath,
Yea! of my Love's that is so dear and gay.
Ah God! Ah God! That dawn should come so
    soon! '

Envoi.

Fair is this damsel and right courteous,
And many watch her beauty's gracious way.
Her heart toward love is no wise traitorous.
Ah God! Ah God! That dawns should come so soon!

Planh

It is of the white thoughts that he saw in the Forest.

WHITE Poppy, heavy with dreams,
    O White Poppy, who art wiser than love,
Though I am hungry for their lips
        When I see them a-hiding
And a-passing out and in through the shadows
—There in the pine wood it is,
And they are white, White Poppy,
They are white like the clouds in the forest of the sky
Ere the stars arise to their hunting.

O White Poppy, who art wiser than love,
I am come for peace, yea from the hunting
Am I come to thee for peace.
Out of a new sorrow it is,
That my hunting hath brought me.

White Poppy, heavy with dreams,
Though I am hungry for their lips
        When I see them a-hiding
And a-passing out and in through the shadows
—And it is white they are—
But if one should look at me with the old hunger in
        her eyes,
How will I be answering her eyes?

50

For I have followed the white folk of the forest.

Aye! It's a long hunting
And it's a deep hunger I have when I see them
      a-gliding
And a-flickering there, where the trees stand apart.

But oh, it is sorrow and sorrow
When love dies-down in the heart.

CHISWICK PRESS: CHARLES WHITTINGHAM AND CO.
TOOKS COURT, CHANCERY LANE, LONDON

BY THE SAME AUTHOR

Personae

*Choicely Printed at the Chiswick Press on fine
paper. Foolscap Octavo, 2s. 6d. net*

SOME EARLY REVIEWS

The Observer says:—"It is something, after all, intangible and indescribable that makes the real poetry. Criticism and praise alike give no idea of it. Everyone who pretends to know it when he sees it, should read and keep this little book."

The Bookman:—" No new book of poems for years past has had such a freshness of inspiration, such a strongly individual note, or been more alive with undoubtable promise."

The Daily Chronicle:—" All his poems are like this, from beginning to end, and in every way, his own, and in a world of his own. For brusque intensity of effect we can hardly compare them to any other work. It is the old miracle that cannot be defined, nothing more than a subtle entanglement of words, so that they rise out of their graves and sing."

From a 3½ page detailed critique, by Mr. Edward Thomas, in *The English Review*:—"He has . . . hardly any of the superficial good qualities of modern versifiers; . . . He has not the current melancholy or resignation or unwillingness to live; nor the kind of feeling for nature that runs to minute description and decorative metaphor. He cannot be usefully compared with any living writers; . . . full of personality and with such power to express it, that from the first to the last lines of most of his poems he holds us steadily in his own pure, grave, passionate world. . . . The beauty of it ('In praise of Ysolt') is the beauty of passion, sincerity and intensity, not of beautiful words and images and suggestions; . . . the thought dominates the words and is greater than they are. Here ('Idyl for Glaucus') the effect is full of human passion and natural magic, without any of the phrases which a reader of modern verse would expect in the treatment of such a subject. This admirable poet. . . ."

The Oxford Magazine:—"This is a most exciting book of poems."

The Evening Standard :—" A queer little book which will irritate many readers."

The Morning Post :—" Mr. Ezra Pound . . . immediately compels our admiration by his fearlessness and lack of self-consciousness."

The Isis (Oxford) :—" This book has about it the breath of the open air, . . . physically and intellectually the verse seems to reproduce the personality with a brief fulness and adequacy. It is only in flexible, lithe measures, such as those which Coventry Patmore chose in his ' Unknown Eros,' and Mr. Pound chooses here that a fully suitable form for the recital of spiritual experience is to be found. Mr. Pound has a true and invariable feeling for the measures he employs . . . this wonderful little book. . . ."

The Daily Telegraph :—" A poet with individuality. . . . Thread of true beauty. . . . lifts it out of the ruck of those many volumes, the writers of which toe the line of poetic convention, and please for no more than a single reading."

Mr. Punch, concerning a certain Mr. Ezekiel Ton :—" By far the newest poet going, whatever other advertisements may say ;" and announced as "the most remarkable thing in poetry since Robert Browning," says :—" He has succeeded where all others have failed, in evolving a blend of the imagery of the unfettered west, the vocabulary of Wardour Street, and the sinister abandon of Borgaic Italy."

Mr. Scott-James, in *The Daily News* :—" At first the whole thing may seem to be mere madness and rhetoric, a vain exhibition of force and passion without beauty. But, as we read on, these curious metres of his seem to have a law and order of their own ; the brute force of Mr. Pound's imagination seems to impart some quality of infectious beauty to his words. . . . With Mr. Pound there is no eking out of thin sentiment with a melody or a song. He writes out of an exuberance of incontinently struggling ideas and passionate convictions. . . . He plunges straight into the heart of his theme, and suggests virility in action combined with fierceness, eagerness, and tenderness. . . . he has individuality, passion, force, and an acquaintance with things that are profoundly moving." Mr. Scott-James begins his half-column review of Mr. Pound's book with a remark that he would "Like much more space in which to discuss his work," and also notes a certain use of spondee and dactyl which "Comes in strangely and, as we first read it, with the appearance of discord, but afterwards seems to gain a curious and distinctive vigour."

LONDON: ELKIN MATHEWS, VIGO STREET, W.

The longest Series of Original Contemporary
Verse in existence

List of the "Vigo Cabinet"
and the "Satchel" Series

LONDON: ELKIN MATHEWS, VIGO STREET, W.

The Vigo Cabinet Series

An Occasional Miscellany of Prose and Verse

Royal 16mo. One shilling net each Part

THE VIGO CABINET SERIES—*continued.*

*Also to be had in cloth, 1s. 6d. net.

₊ Other Volumes in preparation.

The Satchel Series

Fcap. 8vo, cloth, 1s. 6d. *net ; wrapper,* 1s. *net*

THE VISION. (Studies of Mysticism.) By

MRS. HAMILTON SYNGE. With a Photogravure after a Picture by G. F. WATTS, R.A.

CONTENTS: The Vision, Mysticism, The Inward Life, The Subconscious Mind, One in Many, The Ray of Light.

AIRY NOTHINGS: Humorous Verse. By JESSIE

POPE, Author of "Paper Pellets."

EARLY VICTORIAN AND OTHER PAPERS.

By E. S. P. HAYNES, late Scholar of Balliol College, Oxford.

"The author of this book first attracted our attention by his 'Standards of Taste in Art' some few years ago. It was a brief but suggestive essay by one who was obviously that rare bird, a keen and disinterested lover of literature. Detachment from purely literary ideals added a charm to the book. In these new essays this detachment is even more definite. Several of the papers would have a peculiar interest from their subject alone, one study reveals some nineteenth-century characteristic in a manner beyond the reach of any but Samuel Butler's irony."—*Bookman.*

SONGS OF GOOD FIGHTING. By EUGENE

R. WHITE. With a Prefatory Memoir by HARRY PERSONS TABER.

"A book of stirring verse. . . . The most remarkable piece in the volume is the 'Festin d'Adieu,' a short story, which is surely one of the half-dozen finest stories ever written."—*The Bibliophile.*

THE SHADOW SHOW. By A. ST. JOHN ADCOCK.

With Frontispiece by STARR WOOD.

"The deftest and lightest of light verse. . . . Mr. Adcock shows himself very nearly the equal of Hood."—*Morning Leader.*

THE FANCY: a Selection from the Poetical

Remains of the late PETER CORCORAN (*i.e.*, JOHN HAMILTON REYNOLDS, the friend of JOHN KEATS). A verbatim Reprint, with Prefatory Memoir and Notes by JOHN MASEFIELD, and 13 Illustrations by JACK B. YEATS.

"Humorous, and full of a mischievous topical fun . . . delightfully illustrated by Mr. Jack Yeats."—*Manchester Guardian.*

PAPER PELLETS: Humorous Verse. By JESSIE
POPE. Fcap. 8vo, cloth, 1s. 6d. net ; wrapper, 1s. net.

"*Mr. Punch*, who has enjoyed an intimate observation of her talent,
ventures to give a guardian's blessing."—*Punch.*
"It is all bright and merry and sparkling . . . a really witty little
book."—*Vanity Fair.*
"Miss Pope has a dainty touch, and can prick a bubble in the
kindest manner in the world . . . shows great promise of literary dis-
tinction."—*World.*

A MAINSAIL HAUL. (Nautical Yarns). By
JOHN MASEFIELD. With Frontispiece by JACK B.
YEATS.

"Mr. Masefield has the true spirit of the ancient childhood of the
earth. He has the real spirit of the poets, and he has it precisely in
that particular in which the poets and the tellers of fairy tales most
seriously and most decisively differ from the realists of our own day.
Mr. Masefield tells a story that is in itself strange, or splendid, or even
supernatural, but tells it in the common, graphic language of life."—
Mr. G. K. CHESTERTON, in *Daily News.*

ADMISSIONS AND ASIDES. Essays Literary
and Social. By A. ST. JOHN ADCOCK.

"A series of inspiring reflections on events that occur continually
around us, and bears marks of that incisive spirit of introspection which
has characterized this writer's work."—*London Opinion.*
"The work of an essayist with the charm of a poet and the wit and
sense of a delightful prose writer."—*Academy.*

LONDON ETCHINGS. By A. ST. JOHN ADCOCK.

"The most delicate and finished prose work that has so far come
from this popular author's pen."—*Sunday Times.*
"We welcome the frank slightness of these sketches. It is part of a
recognition that the *how* is more than the *how much*, which is new in
English literary art. . . . As slight and clever fragments of observation
'London Etchings' are well done."—*Athenæum.*

THE VIEWS OF CHRISTOPHER. With a
Preface by COULSON KERNAHAN. [*Second Edition.*

"Wholesome, vehement, exacting criticism of men and manners in
general is set down in this dainty book with the frankness, gravity, and
finality of the philosophy of eager youth. . . . It may frankly be
commended *virginibus puerisque* and to the elders. A good book."—
The Month.

LONDON
ELKIN MATHEWS
VIGO STREET, W.